HOW TO
FIND YOUR
JOY
IN A CRAZY,
UPSIDE-DOWN
WORLD

GINGER GRANCAGNOLO, ED.D., D.MIN.

BALBOA.
PRESS
A DIVISION OF HAY HOUSE

Balboa Press books may be ordered through booksellers or by contacting:

Balboa Press
A Division of Hay House
1663 Liberty Drive
Bloomington, IN 47403
www.balboapress.com
1 (877) 407-4847

Print information available on the last page.

ISBN: 978-1-5043-5041-9 (sc)
ISBN: 978-1-5043-5042-6 (e)

Library of Congress Control Number: 2016902133

Balboa Press rev. date: 02/19/2016

CONTENTS

DEDICATION

… to my dearest friend, Carol … who is not only my personal example of REAL JOY, she is and always has been the embodiment of REAL JOY. No matter what experiences life seemed to have brought us, from tragedies to triumphs, we have always been able to find the JOY. Thank you, Carol, for always being such a sparkling JOY-maker.

ACKNOWLEDGMENTS

REAL JOY is meant to be shared! Abundant gratitude to each of you! Our shared joy has made my life so wondrously rich and overflowing with love.

Thank you! Thank you!

Wendy, Carol, Elaine, Sue, Eva, Cina,
Concetta, Debra, Vicki

You have filled my life with endless sparkles!

INTRODUCTION

If you will, please, think of the word JOY and observe your immediate response. What just happened? Did you bubble up into smiles? Or did you frown with thoughts of, "I wish; I don't remember when"?

Okay, let's do it again. This time, bring back a memory of a truly JOY-ful time. Stay focused upon it. Remember as many details as possible. Recall the people, places, colors, aromas, and season. Just stay in these images for a moment and just relax into the splendor of this recollection. Just breathe and melt into this pleasurable reflection.

Isn't it amazing how quickly a happy flashback can cause a shift in the moment? A simple image may seem to be a distant experience, yet when recalled can fill the present with a dazzlingly good feeling that can lift your consciousness into new and exciting possibilities.

Yes, for sure, JOY can be quite powerful. In fact, JOY is power. JOY is a divine spark that spontaneously releases the heart of God from within our own hearts. It's powerful, beautiful, and so often unpredictable.

REAL JOY has its own signature. It is not to be confused with happiness. Happiness, although good and highly regarded, is not the same as JOY. Happiness typically has a cause and effect. For example, happiness is felt when a goal, desire or dream is set forth and achieved – such as, "I will be happy when I start the new job" or "I'll be happy when we move into the house" or "I will be happy when the divorce is final."

In this regard, happiness has a function. Basically, it can fuel us to get from one station in life to another. Conversely, if the desired cause and effect is not achieved, for whatever reason, great unhappiness, perhaps even despair or a sense of powerlessness, can remain.

REAL JOY is different. It doesn't have a beginning or an end. It doesn't have a function in linear time. JOY's purpose does the opposite. It lifts us out of the mundane and sparks us into feelings of awe that are beyond daily reasoning and time and space dimensions. Without explanation, JOY-ful experiences lift us into a moment of sheer heaven. Its power, having been felt deep into the soul, changes us forever.

Who can remain the same after gazing upon the face of their newborn baby for the very first time? Such an experience is JOY in perfection. Such an image remains in the heart and soul transcending all logic as it continuously serves to teach about the incomprehensible grace and wonder of God with every future reflection.

JOY is the presence of God bursting through us as our soul beams onto an experience that is purely divine, i.e., sunrises, sunsets, the genuine and unexpected embrace, connecting glances that speak without words in ways that stir and lighten the heart, quiet visitations in nature, watching as a loved one peacefully sleeps.

JOY teaches us God is here, in and around us, waiting to touch us with timeless heavenly love. JOY is the presence of God that is ever-present even though this reality seems unavailable under the veil of our highly distractible lifestyles.

Despite our whirlwind lives, JOY still remains as just the jolt we need to redirect our focus back into divine truth. JOY and divine truth can be described as the right and left arm of God eagerly ready to embrace us, at any moment, as a loving reminder that heaven is not so far away.

REAL JOY returns us to the soul – the peace of knowing, without words, that we are always safe and loved.

The purpose of this reading is to first explain how and why we lost our JOY (Part One: The Problem). Then we will learn how to regroup our steps (Part Two: The Solution) so we can once again be more equipped for staying open for JOY, REAL JOY, ready and able at any moment.

I pray this reading awakens your heart and heals your soul. I pray it reignites your JOY to live, love, and be loved in the simplest way, making every day quite extraordinary!

> *"The Lord has done great things for us, and we are filled with joy."*

Psalm 126:3

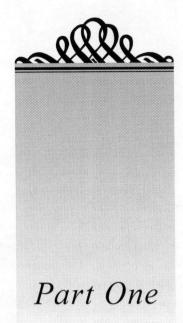

Part One

THE PROBLEM

CHAPTER ONE

HOW DID WE GET SO CRAZY?

As I was cleaning out a dresser drawer recently, I came upon an old photo of my parents. The photo was taken when they were seated at a dinner table with other family members. At this time, my parents had just become engaged and their mutual gazing into each other's eyes spoke volumes without words. Their love-locked look spoke to me about their hopes, wishes, and dreams as I could feel their presence so alive in that old photo. The table was covered with delectable food ready for feasting. Candles, wine glasses, and squeezed-in seating were all brilliant signs of a happy celebration in the making.

I pondered over this picture that I might soak up its reminiscent healing and loving essence. Every face and gesture captured carried its own private story that my heart still holds and feels robustly. Truthfully, the scene could have been any Sunday, holiday or anytime someone "came over" for dinner. This was our routine and ritual.

As I further thought about those years, which is at least a half of a century ago, I allowed myself to drift more and more into the rhythm and ways of that time. My father worked, as did my grandfathers.

Mothers and grandmothers were home then, managing, caring for all household tasks. We didn't have a lot; we just had each other, our traditions, and rituals. Our recipe for life seemed almost predictable, although no one seemed to mind.

Even though this image may sound like a snapshot from "Pleasantville," our lives were not without issues. My mother's heart carried to her grave the pain of the death of her first child. My maternal grandfather lost everything in the Great Depression. My father lost a brother at an early age due to polio. My great-grandfather could drink too much, even though no one would ever talk about it. And my aunt's "wise guy" husband had a "heavy hand" over her that we also never discussed.

Certainly, it wasn't perfect. No life ever is. Yet we had great love and celebrations. My paternal grandfather, Papa Migo, loved the latest inventions and loved being the first on the block to have each new one as well. I remember clearly when Papa got the newest color TV. Wow! What a celebration that was! At least 20 of us gathered and crowded into the living room to watch, of course, Ed Sullivan. And yes, that did become a Sunday ritual.

Although those times were filled with both trials and triumphs, what I don't remember is the agonizingly rapid pace of life that now is our accepted normal.

It seems our daily mantra has become a struggling internal murmuring that is saying, "it's so hard to just keep up with everything." Since the onset of television, the pace of technology and information obviously has progressed even beyond scientists' and inventors' wildest imaginings. We have moved from one television and a rotary phone in most homes to an iPhone, computer, social media, Instagram, YouTube, Twitter, Facebook, Fitbit, and a must-have device called the Apple Watch. Whew! How did that happen and mostly in the last 20 years?

Over and over, moment to moment, we are now bombarded with information whether we like it or not. Some of the data deluge is useful and allows us to truly become a more global community. Unfortunately, some information is overkill marketing and advertising. Yet perhaps the most detrimental use of technology might be the constant displays of fear-based and violent eruptions in the daily news reports. Certainly some may argue that we need it to remain informed so that we can stay apprised of life's events. This opinion can continue with a defense that demands a need for more information in order to secure and make intelligent decisions concerning family needs, finances, lifestyle adjustments, career choices, and politics, just to mention a few categories.

For sure, there is good evidence that proves the more we can know, the better the discernment and its effectiveness. However, it appears that the information overload into our daily lives may have created an actual addiction. So many of us need the connection to information through constant attachment to our various devices. Through iPhones, iPads, Facebook, and other forms of social media, we seem to be endlessly "checking in and connecting" in cyberspace, even it if isn't truly necessary. Scientific research provides much evidence supporting the reality of just how addicted we may be to the constant attachment to and use of these devices when we observe the behavior of individuals once technology has been removed from their environments for a designated time. The results range from discomfort to anxiety and even dysfunctionality.

Obviously, the answer to our stress-filled lifestyles is not to remove technology or its flow of information. Both are here to stay and advanced innovations are certain.

The concern is who have we become over the last 20 years due to this tech boom? Did we really become better? Did it really help us to connect more? Are we better communicators? Did it make our families and relationships closer? And ultimately, did it make the world a safer place?

These questions are intended to stir our thought process. I am sure there can be doubt and certainty in equal proportions as to the pros and cons of our steadily progressing age of information. In truth, that may not be an issue anyone can ever succinctly clarify. However, what we can do is evaluate how these mammoth changes with all the plusses and minuses have affected us personally.

That is the focus of this writing. Perhaps it's time to look at who we have become as individuals. Are we more joyful? Are we heartfully satisfied? Do we feel safe and grounded? Do we trust there is a Divine Presence within us that can and will direct and guide us regardless of outside daily events?

These are the issues we will address throughout this book. Even though our lives no longer seem to have a routine script or formula, and it can appear to feel like we are swimming in a sea of uncertainty, REAL JOY still exists.

It is my experience and observation that even though the rush of information and our inability to sufficiently process so much in any given day has contributed to our anxieties, fears, and addiction to "staying" informed, the real issue is not technology or its use by itself. The real issue, as I view it, is that through technology our attention has been progressively focused upon what's outside of us so disproportionately that for some our interior beauty and divinity have been either abandoned or viewed as a powerless aspect of ourselves.

Herein lies the core of our joyless lives. The more we focus outside of self, the less we will understand or connect with our inner dimensions of heart and soul.

True invincible power is within us. Our very breath is a divine gift. In every inhalation and exhalation, the Beloved Creator comingles into our cellular tissues. What a JOY-ful moment it is when we merely remember it is a "WHO" that created us and not a "what."

The "Who" within us not only sources us continually, it also knows us by name. Our Creator is the constant Beloved Wisdom waiting in our hearts who wants to show us our true nature and true purpose for living. This Holy One desires to dissolve the illusions of false perceptions, fear, false attachments, and distorted beliefs. The Holy One is the Author of the universe and lives in the center of our being always. However, if we are not focused on the center, we can be very vulnerable to living more in highly distractible lifestyles that simply have no inherent power to keep us safe or JOY-ful. There is no ultimate power in what is finite, only in what is infinite. And the Infinite One lives in the center of our beings, waiting to "connect" so we can know our truth and enjoy a more love-filled life.

The last two decades or more may have created endless scientific advancements, yet they also may have produced detrimental amnesia concerning where our REAL power resides. I believe it is this forgetfulness that has diminished our JOY-ful potential.

Such continued forgetfulness can really make us feel unglued and a little crazy! There is no way we can ever know enough, keep up enough, or process the constant influx of information enough as a means of staying grounded. It is simply impossible to adequately process all the daily data in such a way that brings us to accurate conclusions. This is because so much of what we hear or see is fear-based opinions or manipulated perceptions and therefore is not the truth. Again, so much of this kind of ungrounded information just keeps making us a little crazy!

It takes only a simple act of remembering WHO is at the center of our beings and peace and JOY can flow freely again. As we become more centered from within, false perceptions can fade and clearer wisdom can be reclaimed. What JOY awaits when we choose peace and calm from within! Our energy can be replenished and purposeful motivation for daily activities can be revitalized. If we allow ourselves to stay in a daily routine of shutting out the worldly chatter and shift to an inner quiet, a more balanced perspective about life can be regained. By going into our center in calm silence, we rebuild feeling and staying centered. From this more grounded posturing, JOY can be ignited again!

Remembering the JOY remedy:

* Sit quietly and undisturbed for 5-10 minutes daily. Focus on your breathing in an easy, rhythmic manner as you visualize a glowing, golden light in the center of your chest.
* Then recall a JOY-ful time. Recreate it in your mind as if you are watching a movie.
* Then as you are remembering these moments, repeat to yourself several times, "I am this JOY; I am this JOY!"
* When you are ready to open your eyes, be certain to make a beautiful smile on your face.

"My soul finds rest in God alone;
My salvation comes from him.
He alone is my rock and my salvation.
He is my fortress; I will never be shaken."

Psalm 62:1-2

CHAPTER TWO

OLD VS. NEW: FOR BETTER OR WORSE

Oh, the good ole' days! Such a common reflection! It seems most of us like to take that walk down memory lane. We appear to look back with smiling eyes at the way things used to be. We savor our worn photos, even if they have already been transposed onto DVDs. When family and friends gather for special events, our conversations can easily drift to earlier days and the stories that go along with those more youthful times.

For some, this reminiscent journey is painful. For some of us, it means remembering who's no longer here, who died, and who drifted away. These reflections on the past can lead us to feel that as those days and loved ones have gone, so also has the hope that life now and in the future will hold much real JOY.

Certainly, this can be seen among dispersed families who are now living in distant locations and the elderly, who can feel limited by the absence of family and friends. Some will dispute that early times were clearly better. They will hold fast to their perceptions that times before were easier, less complicated, and more harmonious.

Some may even argue that technology upset the apple cart by making everything move so fast that simplicity has lost its value. They may complain that all these devices, gadgets, and machines have made us function more like robots than humans.

Yet others will proudly boast about how they are learning more than ever. They are actually enjoying the ability to have so much information at such a quick click or a tap on their handheld devices. They are excited about their improved ability to create new businesses and fine tune finances, increase research for personal or professional purposes online 24/7, while they are staying well informed about news, politics, weather, sports, global events, and stock market trends almost at the moment any of it occurs.

There would seem to be evidence for heated debate from both sides of these points of view. At the core, maybe the concern is not which is better or worse, but rather how has the quality of life evolved? With this question as the focus, I would suspect even more pros and cons could be listed.

Even with all the advancements in transportation, commerce, science, medicine, education, space exploration, and technology, are we really any better off as people, individually, within communities, and among nations? Some evidence can confuse or mislead us.

The major issues of racism, gender equality, violence, drugs, corrupt politics, and terrorism that existed sixty or even seventy years ago not only are still present, they have drastically escalated.

So, what's the truth? Are we better or worse than we were before? Have we become more civilized and sophisticated or distinctly more violent and greedy? Is the world safe today or not?

These are pertinent and real questions that will not have any short or easy answers. As decades have rapidly rushed us forward into a new century, we can perceive ourselves as being more fearful than hopeful. We are hammered by the media constantly. We listen all day and night and some follow like it is the only sheriff in town, and they willingly go along with the news of the day as if it were the only rule of the day.

Perhaps this observation brings a better understanding about the reality of life today. As mentioned, there is always so much data buzzing around us day and night. Nonstop information is zipping through cyberspace into our living rooms, devices, and consciousness. We are bombarded by media flow constantly and some still crave more.

With this endless tsunami of information, now stretching over decades, we have become "hooked" to outside stimulation and distractions. The more our focus of attention has remained outside of self, the less focus of attention there has been to the inside of self. To name it specifically, we as a global community may have become more attached to the world and its blurring fear affects than to our interior hearts and souls, which are always radiating in divine peace and truth. The only part of us that is permanent, timeless, reliable, and perfect is our interior. Our inner spirit remains untouched and never contaminated by any opinion. Our interior is the unchanging, uncreated presence of God.

That said, even though it may appear our world has become more chaotic and fearfully unpredictable, this is not, and has never been, the truth. Creation is created by the Creator, who is always, no matter what, LOVE.

Of course, it would be expected that our reaction to this statement might be, "then why are we still a mess?" or "why doesn't God do something about it?" The answers to these inquiries are the same as stated before. God is unconditional – no conditions, no limitations, no interference – and ever-present in full potential within us, all the time.

So, how does this truth apply to the conflicts of life as we see it; namely, how can we rectify a chaotic, upside-down world, and yet trust the awesome power of God that was breathed into us from the moment we were created? The hopeful clarity lies in another truth given by God: We have free will.

Ultimately, all of history is an ongoing story of free will. All events are the result of our choices individually and collectively. History does not have to inherently "repeat itself." It may be in repetitive patterns because we haven't changed our choices. We will "get better" based on our free will to do so, both as individual persons and together as a global community. This is the truth.

The real problem, therefore, is not that the quality of life is not based on past or present. The real problem is whether we will continue to look outside or inside for solutions in order to reclaim life as the Creator intended it to be.

The more our focus of attention remains outside toward world views, strict traditions, government party policies and mores, the more limited we will become. Even Albert Einstein stated a problem cannot be solved at the level that the problem exists. The solution lies in a higher frequency of consciousness and understanding. The solutions we are seeking to our issues, no matter what they may be, already exist in our interior being, which are pure Spirit and the highest frequency of consciousness.

Many are still looking outside themselves for answers. The real solution is to teach, guide, and direct us and others to "go within." Some have said that unless we learn to go within, we will continue to go with-out, living in lack of wisdom rather than an abundance of both self-love and wisdom.

Once we learn to stay in a steady discipline of prayer, quiet, and silent listening meditation, we will become aware of great insights. We will understand our past in new ways. We will embrace our past and present as stepping stones, lessons of forgiveness leading us to victories and greatness. We will understand that the permanent imprint "made in the image and likeness of God" is real. We will feel differently about the ongoing story of our lives because we will have shifted our lens from outside viewing to inside viewing, where we will see our past and present as a series of choices made either in awareness of our true connection to an all-powerful, loving God, or unaware choices based in fear, anger or control.

The more we focus from within ourselves in a dialogue with the Holy Spirit, the more we get to see the whole truth on all levels, including all concerned as well as the "why" of the stories of our lives. Without this inner view, we see only from ego, which is always limited, self-serving, and pushing for some kind of control. Ego looks outward and sees only its own needs and point of view. Soul sees with the eye of God, which always includes all needs, lessons, and desires in equally loving ways. The soul seeks victory in love for all. The ego pushes for victory over someone or something and is never interested in equality.

These perspectives about inner soul focus are always true because they are sourced from God and this is how God expresses Herself through us. Therefore, these views apply all the time, regardless of whether they are applied to a person, neighborhood, state, nation or the world.

What has occurred throughout recorded time is like watching the motion of a pendulum as it swings from all the way left to all the way right. The course of history moves from more outer focus of attention to more inner focus of attention. Perhaps an example of a historical time when humanity may have been more focused upon inwardly spiritually motivated pursuits would be the Renaissance Age. During this time, humanity created magnificent works of art and literature that were almost beyond human understanding. Conversely an example of humanity focusing on more materialistic pursuits maybe noted as the Industrial Revolution. Many favorable and highly practical inventions were created during this time that are still a great benefit to all aspects of life. Greatness was achieved during both of these times, however a balanced living in both spirit and matter as a total society has yet to be accomplished. According to the choices society makes, so go the conditions of life. When a society is not balanced in both inward and outward endeavors many problems can result. An increase in fear can easily manifest when society does not actively connect and utilize its inherent divine potential. As fear escalates in any culture an atmosphere for violence and destruction can unfortunately appear to be a solution when in fact it will only add to the problems of imbalance.

Regardless of the generation, we have all experienced both. In fact, this is part of the divine plan. How else would we really understand or embrace our full capacity of "made in the image and likeness of God" if we didn't get to use our free will in order to truly experience the unconditional love of God that is within (His image) and the choice to act upon that unconditional love (Her likeness) so we can feel likened unto God?

Certainly, individually and collectively, our choices can influence our surroundings. That's why it is essential to stay focused from our "soul-eyes" and not our "ego-eyes." These past several decades have served a great purpose. Yes, there is still much poverty, illness, injustice, and violence. Yet, I view these times as a great awakening. Through advanced technologies, we have all been invited to fast-forward awareness. Technology has exposed everything, positive and negative, fearful and loving, everywhere. We are all seeing what we never were aware of before in both positive and negative ways. We are becoming more and more aware even if we don't want to! This is the blessing. We can't change what we are not aware of. The more we can see ourselves and others differently by using our "soul-eyes," the more we will change into our original blueprint creation of being co-creators with our Creator, and we will recreate heaven on earth as it was intended to be.

No doubt time, inner prayer, forgiveness, and patience are needed. For better or worse, we already have the power to allow it to be so, if we would just steadfastly go within.

Every time we experience our inner wisdom, we actually change our energetic frequency to more and more pure love. Love changes everyone and everything for both the givers and the receivers. This shift opens endless doorways to REAL JOY even in the simplest ways. Simply stated, love and JOY are already within us, waiting to be felt and shared, always there, in the current moment, now!

Remembering the JOY remedy:

* Sit quietly and undisturbed for 5-10 minutes. Focus on your breathing in an easy, rhythmic manner as you visualize a glowing, golden light in the center of your chest.

* Remember a favorite place, routine, relationship, or tradition that may no longer be a part of your present life.

* Focus on the pleasant, loving feelings until you feel like you are really there, until that past memory feels really present.

* Focus on "how did this situation shape me into becoming a greater version of being me?"

* Thank each person involved, including yourself, for all the choices you made, even if some choices didn't seem positive at the time. All choices enhance the development of free will.

* Repeat over and over, "I am grateful for the past because it has helped me to become a better me. I am JOY-filled now and always. I am better than yesterday. Amen.

"We know that in all things God works for the good of those who love Him, who have been called according to His purpose."

Romans 8:28

CHAPTER THREE

COPING, CARING, AND FIXING

Needless to say, as the pace of activities, tasks, and responsibilities has increased, so too has the physical, mental, and emotional effort accelerated in order to maintain some stability in our lives. This observation can make it appear that the goal of any day is to simply cope and keep moving.

If this is the truth, how could we ever expect to find JOY and live JOY-fully? Is seeking JOY just for a child's imagination? Is it a reasonable request to seek balance of "work and play" in our adult lives and, even more important, is it attainable?

Yes! Yes! Yes! JOY is REAL and attainable and so is a balanced life. The issue is not if we can recreate a better rhythm for our lives, the issue is how.

Most of us have been influenced by the notion that knowledge is power. Certainly this idea has been extremely reinforced through the ongoing age of information that we live in. From this premise, our problem-solving formula mostly proceeds from "get knowledge first and peace will follow." With this formula as a guiding template, most of us will go on a fact-finding mission, to a greater or lesser degree, of information according to the problem at hand, searching for the correct set of answers so that after organizing the facts, a viable solution and peace will then be the reward.

Please note knowledge can be powerful, yet it is not in and of itself power as Source.

If we allow an alternative to the above-mentioned formula of knowledge first, peace results, a very unique process can unfold that promises oneness with the Source of ALL of everything that is. This alternative doesn't deny the necessity for good knowledge, but rather calls for a shift in the priority of what to do first in order to obtain the ultimate Source of information that can direct us to an ultimate solution, including the highest good for all concerned.

The shift needed that can allow the flow of the totality of Divine Wisdom is this: Seek first the kingdom of heaven and everything else will follow. And the kingdom is within.

When we choose to resolve concerns from this best-case scenario, we need to change the order of how we approach the issue. Instead of finding facts first, then peace will follow, real effectiveness is obtained by doing the opposite. To receive the best results, the formula to follow is this: Identify the concern, go within, listen and wait, listen and wait, even write it down, then follow. In the divine world, the formula is to seek peace first and wisdom will follow.

If we think about these two approaches for a moment, we can begin to understand why the latter choice makes better sense. From the world approach, we may be plunging nervously into an ocean of information, hoping to find the correct data to help us solve a concern. Even if we find information, we can further spin in waves of confusion and misinterpretations. This process can mostly add fear instead of attempting to diminish it.

The divine approach, however, begins with the single intent of seeking peace first. This approach asks us to remember that all that God is, is always within us, never partial or conditional, no matter what. When we follow in the divine model, we connect the very heart of God that is ever-present in our own hearts by merely breathing. Every breath in and out guides us away from fear and uncertainty and into peace and the insights needed to direct us toward the path of our highest good. Yes, we do need discipline with this prayerful technique since we most probably are already firmly versed in the worldly model of facts first and hopefully peace will follow.

If we continue to stay diligent with the divine approach, we will discover that we are truly created to live with solutions like stepping stones that help us to move into a better quality of living and loving through a better ongoing inner relationship with God.

The divine approach is not only for resolving issues, it is a lifestyle approach that inherently will create balance in our everyday lives because with repetition, we can learn to stay anchored to the Source of Love and Truth. The insights we receive can reveal the untruths, false opinions, control patterns, and fear-based perceptions that the worldview seems to endlessly perpetuate.

If we truly desire to find our JOY and then live a JOY-ful life, we must redefine how we deal with conflicts. Conflicts are a part of life and may always be a part of our lives. The concern here again is not that we have challenges but how we approach them. From the worldly model, we can often feel like we are existing day by day hoping to manage events as well as possible. We wait for happy times and fear they are few and fleeting. The worldly view for living can be filled with anxiety about how to cope and care for loved ones, while fearing what might need to be fixed next. It can keep us feeling vulnerable or even powerless to effectively be in charge of our lives.

To desire to find our JOY, we must address the reality that life has challenges. However, from the divine model, every challenge has a function and a purpose, and events are not random.

Every time we go within, we are invited to see with new eyes. We are invited to experience the divine essence from the Creator's truth and not our own distortions or incomplete perceptions. In the silence and light from within our hearts, we experience the Holy Logos. The Holy Logos as defined by mystics and contemplatives in many religions is the divine ordering factor of the universe. It is the sacred glue of every living aspect of life, seen and unseen. It is Divine Intelligence, the Oneness, and the Cosmic Whole. The Holy Logos is the very air we breathe. It is Pure Love, Truth, and Order. The Logos cannot be understood or experienced from our physical sensory system. It can be experienced from the inner dimensions of our inner soul-senses. Through quiet, prayerful breathing, we can feel our innate oneness with our Beloved Source and the unconditional love of God can freely flow, helping us to see and feel the truth about ourselves and our life's circumstances. Truly, we are never disconnected from God any more than a single ray of sunshine can break off from the sun itself. And just as the fullness of the sun expresses itself equally through each brilliant ray, so too God continually expresses Herself through us, through every breath we take. Our human eyes can deceive us and cause the illusion of separation from the Light. In this false sense of separation, we can feel alone, confused, and somehow in a constant darkness trying to figure out how to stay safe.

Yet, when we close our human eyes and allow the Holy Logos to reveal itself, we can remember: We are always one in Him, with Him, and through Him. The Holy Logos is the "I am that I am." When we return to this soul-felt truth, life is no longer viewed as a string of disjointed events or a series of haphazard circumstances. It is no longer a luck-of-the-draw existence mixed with some loving and JOY-ful moments. Through a daily connection with the inner "I am that I am," we can participate in life from the most mundane experiences to high-peak epiphanies while observing the constant unfolding process of a divine plan. Through the repeated routine of prayerful meditation, we can learn to watch the cause and effect aspects of life while sensing our inner voice for the why's and how's. Every trial and triumph can be experienced as it was meant to be, woven together with the unified purpose of teaching us to know, love, and trust God. Every moment can be embraced for its true function instead of our constant fearful insecurities that will always contaminate our ability to feel REAL JOY.

With a new prayerful routine of silent listening, we can recreate how we live away from rushing to complete tasks and duties and into witnessing the hand of God moving through us and even carrying us, at times. Each day can bring us great love and wisdom. When this shift is made, we can be released from the illusory entrapment of time, into a peaceful, more calm and confident flow as we observe the hidden beauty of any day as it unfolds.

With this daily routine, we can hear and feel messages from God in our hearts. We can remain grounded in the moment, embraced in the safety of God. From challenges to victories, we can feel the wisdom of the divine continuously expressing Her radiant Self in all that we do, say, think, and feel. We are safe, held in the heart of the Creator who lovingly designed us. We see JOY in the moment. We see JOY as we watch God express Himself through us.

Remembering the JOY remedy:

* Sit quietly and undisturbed for 5-10 minutes. Focus on breathing in an easy, rhythmic manner as you visualize a glowing, golden light in the center of your chest.

* As you are relaxing, visualize your day/night activities. Visualize each activity as you desire it to be. Surround the event and all involved in bright, golden Light. Then release it to God, saying, "In Your Holy Light, allow this to be according to the highest good of all concerned. Infuse me with Your Wisdom by day/night so I can see Your loving ways. Thank you. Amen."

* Write down any questions, concerns, or challenges that are of particular priority. Go within to the golden Light in your chest and ask for your concerns to be seen on a large screen. Keep visualizing the concerns on the wide screen as if you are watching a movie of your own making. Then ask for any guidance, direction, or solution that you might need. Trust your impressions. Feel these impressions as peaceful whispers or insights. When you are ready, open your eyes and write down your experiences.

* Repeat this affirmation at least 10 times for 30 days. If you skip or miss a day, start over. Repeating the affirmation for 30 days brings powerful results.

* Affirmation: "I am determined to see myself differently. I am determined to see my life as JOY-filled as God intended for it to be. Amen."

"Let us then approach the throne of grace with confidence, so that we may receive wisdom and find grace to help us in our time of need."

Hebrews 4:16

CHAPTER FOUR

BUSY LIVES AND BROKEN HEARTS

It has been said that each generation carries with it its own unique tragedies. These past several decades have certainly resonated with many devastations, including terrorism, catastrophic weather patterns, children killing children in school shootings, bombings in public places, and threatening viruses and health scares, to name a few.

Let it be stated that the listing of these tragedies is not intended to enhance our fears and sadnesses. Instead, it is meant to acknowledge that which is evident, and then to provide a better remedy for coping with and understanding the violence and imbalances that are so prevalent in our daily lives.

These present-day pressures can cause us to become confused, resentful, frustrated, hopeless or even numb. We may not know where to go for solace and the truth. The media is often contradictory and our religious beliefs can often stir more judgment than peace.

Where can we go to find sensibility and hopeful remedies? If we look to a very simple metaphor with a bit of science, perhaps we can gain a better perspective. Imagine that we are faced with the task of vacuuming a large pool that hasn't been cleaned in a long time. The surface portion of the water may appear somewhat clear, yet we can see the dirty sediment at the bottom. We begin to vacuum the bottom, assuming once we vacuum the entire length of the pool, the job will be done and all will be ready for expectant swimmers. The more we vacuum, however, the pool becomes murkier and murkier. So much dirt and unforeseen slime now is rising to the surface. The pool is completely cloudy and grimy, and it has become obvious that this cleaning is going to take much longer than anticipated.

If we apply the imagery along with a simple scientific fact (all living organisms heal from the inside out) to the earth and her evolutionary process, we may begin to shift in our understanding about what has been occurring over the past several decades. The earth is a living organism and at her core is a self-regulating organism just like any other living organism. Mother earth is always regulating herself for the sake of stability. She continues to do whatever is necessary to keep herself balanced, which of course includes cleaning up what we have done to her, such as disrespecting nature, neglecting her value, and abusing her gifts. Thus, we have produced many, many decades of negativity and imbalances on earth that can be likened to the toxic residue in the pool that has been ignored for some time. Mother Nature will always do whatever is necessary to maintain herself and us in the evolutionary process of God's commission for all creation and its inhabitants, even though humanity has been irresponsible to her. As Mother Nature is an expression with the Holy Spirit, lessons can be learned and wisdom will prevail. It is the promise of our Creator that we would have all of life and have it abundantly. Yet we need to learn through God's nature of love and not the human egoic ways of greed and force. These selfish human ways are the cause of the worldly toxicity at every level, and therefore it is up to us to correct it and clean it up, both in our own individual lives and in the global community as well. Creation innately functions in Godliness. Obviously, humanity is still learning how to align with Holy Mother Nature.

Until we understand our clean-up responsibilities, we will erroneously believe that worldly conditions are random. With this distorted thinking, we will remain powerless to effectively change anyone or anything for goodness sake. With this toxic false assumption, we will remain hopeless, joyless, and broken-hearted about the fate of ourselves and the world.

Regardless of the severity of personal conditions or worldly conditions, we are never powerless. Power is always waiting within us and so is the free will to use our divine spark at any moment.

We can heal our disappointments, hurts, grief, and illusory fears. We can heal our broken hearts, and we need to go deep into our hearts in order to do so. We need to choose to heal ourselves. Making this firm decision does not imply that we initially need to understand the process of healing or even to trust it. The first step is making the choice to be whole, free, peaceful, and joyful again. This decision must be a full commitment that is reinforced daily by congruent words, emotions, and behavior. No fleeting whim to feel better will suffice. Once this decision becomes well integrated into our fiber, we can begin a process that will reconstruct our perceptions about our lives, and even the world, so that we can realign our awareness with Holy Mother Nature. Then we can embrace how she is regulating our experiences so we can purge old patterns that are self-destructive and reclaim our divine inheritance to be God-like and feel REAL JOY again.

As certain as day follows night, our sense of self and life will shift to a greater calm the more we rely upon inner peace and wisdom. It does take courage and daily commitment to see with the eyes of God rather than latching on to public opinion and virtual hearsay. As we continue to choose "to be in the world, but not of it," along with "seek first the kingdom of heaven and everything else will follow," and "the kingdom is within," the sense of our micro world and the macro world will begin to have clarity. We will then be able to embrace a more certain purpose about who we really are, where we have been, and new possibilities for who we can become. It does take patience and discipline, and it is always worth the effort.

Remembering the JOY remedy:

* Write in a journal any upsets, fears, heartaches, loss, or disappointments you may have experienced recently or in the past. Write a list of patterns or habits that you have that are not in your best interest, yet which seem to continue.
* Sit quietly and undisturbed for 10-15 minutes. Focus on breathing in an easy, rhythmic manner as you visualize a glowing Light in the center of your chest.
* As you are relaxing, recall an experience that causes negative feelings in you or a negative habit that is still lingering. Allow yourself to visualize the experience or habit on a wide screen.
* As you are observing, ask the Light of God from within you: "Why did this need to happen? What was Your purpose? What was I supposed to learn from it? How can this experience help me to be more God-like? Why am I still choosing this negative habit? What am I holding on to?"
* Continue to stay focused on the golden Light and, if you choose to, allow all hurts, negative emotions and behaviors to be absorbed into a huge ball of White Light. When you are ready, ask God to bring the ball of Light that now contains all your negative emotions and thoughts up and away from you and to draw it into the center of the universe where it will be completely transformed into a thousand sparkles. Say "thank you, Lord," and then ask that every cell of your being be transmuted into a higher frequency of peace, wisdom, and REAL JOY.
* Write in your journal any reflections from this peaceful meditation. Repeat as often as you desire.

"'Though the mountains be shaken and the hills be removed, yet my unfailing love for you will not be shaken nor my covenant of peace be removed'" says the Lord, who has compassion on you."

Isaiah 54:10

Part Two

THE PROMISE

CHAPTER FIVE

"WHERE ARE YOU, LORD?"

If you have been engaged in some conversations about religion or spirituality lately, you may have heard various comments of concern or discontentment. Some may feel disinterested or disappointed with their familiar practices. They may say they are dull and mostly do not pertain to the personal plight of everyday living. Others may say they simply attend rituals out of habit and that they are not certain of any real growth in spirit or any tangible benefits. Still some may say their faith and prayer practices keep them safe and grounded. There are also some who have abandoned their traditions and have found more solace in yoga, gardening, chanting, Qi Gong, or simply helping others.

No matter how we choose to seek God, it appears that we all can relate to the universal question, "Where are you, Lord?"

Often the question is a deep cry from the pit of our soul. Sometimes, it is a silent plea internally uttered as a response to some experience of injustice. Regardless of the prompting, our soul already knows God since we are truly spiritual beings having human experiences. Our human overcoat can cause a kind of amnesia about who we really are. Yet the fact still remains we are always and forever connected to our Source, which is God. Whenever we post the question about where is God, we may actually be asking to be jarred back into our true reality of unity in the spirit. We may have gotten so distracted or absorbed into three-dimensional living that we may have forgotten about the invisible divine glue of all life. We may have forgotten the obvious. We may have lost sight of the truth that the very gift of breathing is God, breathing through us moment to moment. God is like the A.I.R. we breathe, **a**lways **i**n **r**each.

So, let's pause, right now in this moment, to reconnect to God by remembering Her presence as we breathe. Place your hand over your heart, close your eyes, and focus on an image of God that you are comfortable with. Notice a calm peace that just begins to flow through your whole body. This peace is God, and His safety and wonders are always available to us and are as close as every inhalation and exhalation.

God is everywhere, at all times, ever-present, inside and outside of us simultaneously. In fact, it is quite accurate to say there is no place that God is NOT. This recognition is certainly easy to observe while we are relaxing by a beach, a lake, or a mountain view during our favorite season or at our favorite vacation place. However, it can be difficult to acknowledge when we are stuck in traffic, late for a plane departure, or if we just found out we've been laid off from work. Yet, even in the most devastating events, God is always present.

Perhaps one of the most horrifying events that we can all relate to is the terrorist attack to our country on 9-11. It was traumatic and shook us to the core. Even though this event and its human carnage was truly devastating, there were endless stories of Godly love demonstrated by the heroics of countless people everywhere. God was there in every act of compassion, every shed tear, and every grieving heart. So many lives ended that day, yet so many more lives were changed forever. Private stories of courage and unimaginable strength pushed so many families into a deeper appreciation of their loved ones and maybe even of God Himself. And certainly, there are some who can only cling to the pain and have remained there ever since.

Everyone has a choice about how he or she will respond to a situation. Regardless of how difficult or tragic the event may be, it's still a choice we can make. Circumstances will continue to occur and they may be perceived as good or bad. And the power of choice is up to the individual. We can choose to stay locked in the negative or seek to find the good. No matter what, God's presence is permanently alive and available, inside and outside of ourselves. If we seek something positive, we can align ourselves to a Christ consciousness and find a new value in the experience that ultimately can improve the quality of our lives.

Every experience beckons this invitation. Will we respond with the mind and heart of our spiritual selves and therefore stay connected to God's wisdom and love, or will we respond using only our human senses and therefore slip into falsehoods, limitations, and deepened fears? God is present in either one of those choices. The issue is that we won't be able to feel or access Her power if we respond from an egoic aspect of self.

God is and always will be in us, among us, and expressing through us. The dilemma, therefore, is not where God is, but rather where is our focus at any given moment? The more we focus upon our supernatural connection to God, the more we can experience the supernatural qualities of perfect wisdom, love, abundance, and REAL JOY.

Focus is the compass for a quality life. Whatever we focus upon automatically increases. With this in mind, it becomes evident that if we seek to see and feel the good in ourselves, others, and all experiences, we will receive it. Focus can make any day a miracle day. Albert Einstein once said, "We either believe everything is a miracle or nothing is a miracle. Either way will determine our experience."

REAL JOY is always available since God is always present. The miracle is experienced as we shift our focus to our spiritual eyes of the heart and seek to see God's love and wisdom in everything and everyone. Even if we can only accomplish this a few moments a day, if we persist, a dynamic shift in awareness of just how great the power of God really is can occur. The power is always breathing within us. The recognition of this reality is truly a JOY-filled miracle.

God's power and love are everywhere. If we would just choose to stay focused upon it, we would, in fact, become it!

Remembering the JOY remedy:

* As you are drifting into sleep, repeat this affirmation several times for 30 nights: "I am JOY, and God's JOY is always flowing within me." The results are amazing.

* Take 15 minutes daily and connect to some aspect of nature, such as sunrise, sunset, flowers, listening to rain, observing shapes in clouds, quiet time with pets, listening to birds, watching the ocean waves. Focus on how it feels in your heart to observe the beauty in nature. Connecting to nature is connecting to God.

* As you are conversing with someone, imagine a beam of light connecting from your heart to his or her heart and silently repeat to yourself, "This light is God's love in us and through us." Your experience with others will greatly improve.

* Before entering into a workplace, important meeting, or conversation, especially if it can be perceived as a difficult situation, imagine each person involved and sense a golden light in the center of each person's chest. Then repeat the word "Namaste" three times silently as you focus upon each person involved, including yourself. Namaste can be translated as "the God within me blesses the God within you." Repeating Namaste while focusing upon each allows the highest good for all concerned to be released.

* At the start of each day, repeat this affirmation three times: "There is great JOY coming to me today. Thank you, God."

"The Lord will guide you always; He will satisfy your needs in a sun-scorched land and will strengthen your frame. You will be like a well-watered garden, like a spring whose waters never fail."

Isaiah 58:11

CHAPTER SIX

TEACH ME TO TRUST

A true and loyal friend is a blessing forever. This kind of bond always brings comfort, strength, and REAL JOY. When we are with our loyal friend, we feel better and more alive. It never seems to matter what we are doing or what adventure might be calling us at a moment's notice. In fact, we are not really concerned about the end results. We simply and quite naturally are just enjoying the time together. The peace and loyalty we share together makes us feel safe. These experiences teach and expand our consciousness and our ability to love ourselves and one another. A true loyal friendship is a timeless treasure. Hopefully, we have had the gift of this kind of friend.

If we reflect upon this loyal friendship for a moment, a new perspective about unconditional love can be gained. When we are bonded in a loyal friendship, we innately maintain a sense of security with this person. We know without reservation that if we need assistance, comfort, or advice for any reason, our loyal friend can be counted on. As soon as we invoke that friend's help, we almost simultaneously can feel in our hearts that it's done. We instinctively feel it's all going to be okay.

We can rely on these inner feelings because our friendship bond has withstood the test of life's trials and triumphs and the friendship remained honest and caring through it all. What a gift to behold!

The qualities and virtues witnessed between loyal friends, although sometimes seemingly rare, are actually within everyone. These blessed connections are the expressions of God's unconditional love and wisdom being freely exchanged between the individuals. Each person feels the loyalty and they simply just trust one another. The trust bond is like knowing without knowing, and the power of the commitment between these two friends is palatable to others who know them.

This kind of trust is not only a precious gift between friends, it is the divine jewel that God is always offering to us. Her love and wisdom is all inclusive and certainly beyond all human understanding. Divine trust is the ultimately loyal friendship with God. It cannot and will not fail us, ever.

If we are going to be really honest with ourselves, even though we may crave such a secure and loyal friendship with God, we may still be asking how this can be achieved. Please note asking that question elicits the process needed to spark a real trust in the power of God.

Our Creator is our constant lover, protector, and confidant. This is God's nature. The Divine Creator of all the universe is and always will be the ever-constant life force of pure love. All expressions of God throughout creation are always vibrating with Her pure essence, even if we don't see it, feel it, or believe it. The full capacity of God remains the same, regardless of our fickle opinions. Therefore, we can trust God to always be perfectly loving. God is always perfectly

God. His part of the divine friendship is reliable and as certain as sky. It is our side of the friendship that can be flighty and unpredictable.

Real trust lessons are best learned by changing our opinions of ourselves. Real trust in God begins when we accept that we are good and lovable all the time because we were designed, created, and remain connected to the Divine Matrix who is the perfection within us! Imagine if you will, that our DNA has a spiritual chromosome that innately knows the best curriculum for our lives and always seeks to fulfill it. In fact, this Divine Intelligence is contained within all living, breathing creatures. It is alive and flourishing in all aspects of nature. For example, a tiny grass seed, when properly nourished, automatically "knows" how to become beautiful, elegant green grass. It didn't have to study how to be grass, or hope to become grass. It just grew into what it was meant to be. It didn't and couldn't become anything else! There was never a fear or question that it might become a rock, corn, or a chipmunk. Its specific innate curriculum calls for beautiful, elegant green grass, and so it is! The only variable is how well it gets nourished.

These truths are parallel to our own. Our spiritual curriculum is set to become God-like. How well we nourish that seed is ours for the choosing. Trusting in our inherent oneness to God and His steadfast love for us will always nourish the seed of self-love and the soul's natural desire to become God-like.

Trust in God increases as we remember who we are by nature instead of how experiences may have reshaped us. Our lives are a constant collection of win-lose events that were never meant to define us. The continuum of the dualistic responses to life's situations was designed to awaken us to our intrinsic godly nature that never changes. The more we seek to rely upon that which is intrinsically good and beautiful, the more we can drop our limiting opinions and fear-based realities in favor of God's Holy Curriculum. We therefore can trust the process of life and witness many miracles as we watch it unfold day by day. In this shift, we can relax. Our Holy loyal friend is REAL and will never leave us!

Trust in God, who is your REAL JOY!

Remembering the JOY remedy:

* Set aside at least one day a week, whenever possible, and make NO plans for that day. Allow any opportunity to arise and choose only that which feels the most JOY-ful. This can help you to trust your natural instincts for JOY.

* Write a list of any particular projects, goals, issues, or even conflicts. List them as desires without specific outcomes. One example might be improved communication among family members and loved ones. Then imagine giving the list to God and saying thank you. Repeat this daily for 30 days. Do nothing else. Observe how situations change for the better without you "doing" anything. God's love never fails.

* Allow 10-15 minutes three times weekly when you can be quiet and undisturbed. It is also recommended for you to be situated in nature whenever that is possible. As you are sitting quietly, imagine God, Jesus, or the Holy Spirit, according to your desire, to be sitting with you. Then ask the question, "Why don't I trust you?" Wait, listen, and observe your experience. Then, when you are ready, ask, "Please remove all falsehoods and hurts so I can feel your love, so I can trust our friendship."

"As for God, his way is perfect. The word of Yahweh is true. He is a shield to all those who take refuge in him."

Psalm 18:30

CHAPTER SEVEN

HAPPY AND HEALING

In a typical survey, a usual question might be, "What do you desire most in life?" Most of the responses select one or all of the following: health, wealth, and happiness, and maybe not in any particular order. These are clearly desirable goals at any point in life. Yet, when we witness someone who has genuinely created a lifestyle including these aspects, we can become judgmental towards that person or ourselves. We may project undue criticism, such as "he inherited money, so it's not really his own earnings" or "sure, it's easy to be happy when you're wealthy." We may feel unwarranted self-criticism, such as "I don't have that kind of luck or intelligence; I am stuck with just maintaining what I have."

The worldly understanding concerning these desirable goals is often that they are products or plateaus to achieve and try to hold onto.

From a spiritual point of view, all three of these are in fact natural states or conditions given by God and are aspects of a natural, well-balanced life. In God's eyes, it's "normal" to experience life as an ongoing process of health, wealth, and happiness. This is so because balance is God's natural experience. Therefore, it is ours as well by divine inheritance. Our natural condition is rooted in God's unconditional, limitless life force. More clearly stated, God has no needs or lacks. Therefore, being one with this divine abundance, our Creator's spiritual imprint is always vibrating and flowing through us with the same divine balance and abundance.

Without awareness of this truth, we can easily get stuck in the needs and fears of life as if we were only a body. Without access to our true inner nature, we can become confined in a thought process of time entrapment, aging, and the loss of control over how to "manage" our lives.

The more we remember who we really are at our spiritual core, the more we can recreate our lives into daily balance and abundance as God intended. In order to properly achieve this balance, we need to change our perspective about our life's goals. We need to flip an internal switch so we can reclaim our power through all our activities. Happiness and healing are fundamentally part of our everyday process. They are attitudes that can continuously direct us back into our spirit centers so we can maintain a "God view" of whatever occurs in any given day, instead of a "human view," which will always be limited and vulnerable to falsehoods and fear.

An excellent understanding about our daily process of maintaining happy and healing attitudes is a main theme in Eckhart Tolle's books, "The Power of Now" and "A New Earth." He describes our process of living as a constant swaying from our "pain body" to our "spirit body." Any time we are experiencing discomfort, stress, anxiety or any condition that makes us feel powerless, Tolle states we shifted out of our natural spirit center and into our false perception that we are only a body, and we therefore experience fear resulting in the feelings of pain. Tolle explains that the remedy for getting out of the imprisoned pain body is to change our focus back into the Holy center rooted in our hearts and souls. He suggests we maintain our awareness in the moment, moment by moment, and with eyes of gratitude. Whenever we are experiencing peace, we are in our spirit center. From this place, awareness and truth naturally become apparent. We are not a body only. We are spirit in a body and only spirit is the power, source, and balance of all life. Basically, our experiences are either coming from fear, the isolated pain body, or from love, the all-encompassing peace body that feels the oneness with God.

Some of the skills needed to help us remain in our peace body as often as possible are prayerful meditation, gratitude, and forgiveness. Prayerful meditation disciplines will keep us close to our spirit center and help retrain how we understand ourselves, life, and God, Herself. The more we meditate, the deeper the relationship with the Holy Spirit, who teaches us about wisdom and the continuity of life's purpose. The more we engage in prayerful meditation, the more life just makes sense.

As we gain skillful and insightful eyes, the wonder of God becomes more evident. We can see and feel JOY more readily, and gratitude about everything can become a natural and fluid response regardless of what may be occurring. The miracle of gratitude is that it automatically anchors us into the NOW and the eternity is the NOW! Whenever we are in heartfelt gratitude, we are moved into another dimension of knowing. We get it! The before, during, and after about some experience makes sense now. We are fulfilled. We thank God for the before, during, and after because somehow it made us better. It made us remember who we really are. In that sacred moment of gratitude, we are wholly healed in the eternal NOW.

What a REAL JOY! We didn't plan how a particular experience

was going to turn out. Somehow, through prayerful meditation and gratitude attitudes, we got out of our fearful pain body and reclaimed our true peace body. Even though these experiences are not constant, it is certainly worth the effort so that living in our peace body can be more normal and frequent than occasional and random. In fact, Eckhart Tolle believes that learning to live from our peace body is living in the eternal NOW and that feels like heaven!

Perhaps our daily activities are designed to give us opportunities to remember the eternal NOW as we can remember heaven is always near and within us. This can only be realized if we are willing to let go of the past. The past chains us to our pain body. It offers no remedy. The more we analyze it, relive it, and hold onto it, the more pain we experience. The past has no power to heal us by itself. This brings us to the third skill needed to maintain a happy and healing life. We need to learn forgiveness.

Forgiveness does not mean it didn't happen or that the hurt wasn't experienced. Forgiveness means we understand why it happened from our spirit eyes and not our human eyes. Forgiveness is the gift we give ourselves so we can return to our peace body and feel heavenly truth and love again. Forgiveness keeps us whole and empowered, not because we are right and they are wrong. Forgiveness opens the doorway to our godliness like no other experience. We need to forgive ourselves and others so we can be set free from the painful judgment cycle. In our humanness, judgment seems normal. It is easy to vacillate between who or what is good or bad all day. Yet, in the judgment habit, there is never freedom.

Every act of forgiveness is an invitation to feel the unconditional love of God and know it is real and for everyone. When we forgive, the shackles of useless guilt and shame are banished. When we forgive, we are face to face with God and are recreated in His love.

We are returned to our heavenly state again. As we are reshaped back into our original blueprint of perfect truth and love, we are humbled and exalted by the power of God, who has carried us through so many trials that we might truly feel the triumph of His awesome love for us. Forgiveness is the pinnacle of godly love in human experiences. Forgiveness heals both the givers and the receivers. Forgiveness is God's ongoing love in action, bringing heaven to earth, once again. Oh, the happy, healing heart who can forgive!

Remembering the JOY remedy:

* Sit quietly and undisturbed for 10-15 minutes. Close your eyes and focus upon the radiant golden light in the center of your chest.

* Allow the light to increase and feel a calm begin to flow throughout your body.

* Ask the Holy Spirit to guide and direct you throughout this prayerful meditation. Ask yourself, "Where do I feel pain or discomfort right now?" Then focus upon that area of pain or discomfort and ask the Holy Spirit to encircle that area and fill it with light. Simply remain focused upon the light as it fills and bathes that area. Repeat quietly to yourself, "Return me to total peace. Holy Spirit Light, return me to total peace." Observe your experience and write down any reflections. Repeat as often as desired. This prayerful meditation can help to shift you back into feeling happy and healing.

* Write down any experiences, recent or past, that you feel may need to be forgiven. Be certain to include experiences of self-judgment and guilt. Then sit quiet and undisturbed for 10-15 minutes. Close your eyes and imagine you are sitting with God, Jesus or the Holy Spirit, according to your desire. Sense the light of the Creator bathing you. Recall the experience that may need to be forgiven. Then ask, "Lord, why did this need to happen? What is Your purpose for this experience?" Then wait and listen. Then ask, "Lord, show me what I need to do, say, think or feel that all may be forgiven." Then wait and listen. Then ask, "Lord, allow your ways to become mine that all might be set free now." Repeat as often as desired. Write

down your reflections. Forgiveness can be a long process. Be patient. God always loves you.

* At the beginning of day, sense a huge, radiant, happy face smile in your heart. Focus upon it again throughout the day. Repeat this affirmation several times as you focus upon the happy face smile in your heart: "I am happy and grateful for all that this day has to offer me. I am safe. I am loved." Repeat as often as possible. Write the affirmation down for easier recall. Attitude is powerful. Gratitude attitude works like magic!

"'I will heal my people and will let them enjoy abundant peace and security,' says the Lord."

Jeremiah 33:6

CHAPTER EIGHT

JOY TO THE WORLD

REAL JOY is always available! REAL JOY is, in fact, always present in the life force of God, who breathes within us. REAL JOY needs only the cultivation and preparation of our attitudes and disciplines so that at any moment JOY can be felt. Staying in waiting for the sacred to be released is the holiest posture we can achieve. So much becomes evident when we do. As we allow any moment to open into a JOY moment, we experience an enlivening energy like no other. We become one with God's love and Her eternal NOW. Our consciousness expands into the wonders of God's universe. In REAL JOY, we know we are loved. In REAL JOY, we remember God is love.

These moments change our past, our present, and our future. The story of our life can take on a new value and a new direction. We can let go of the confinements of our yesterdays because the JOY of the moment reteaches us that no part of the past was in any form a mistake, a regret or a failure. In the moment of JOY, we can reinvent our path for the future with more hope and grounded spiritual stamina than ever before.

Whenever REAL JOY bursts through the mundane, we become one with our own immortality. Some sense of the divine comes forth and illuminates the truth needed to dissolve the most pressing fear lodged in the illusory mind of every human being. When we are lifted into the spontaneity of REAL JOY, we feel the timelessness of life and the myth of death as we knew it fades away.

REAL JOY purges the false perceptions about our bodily existence because REAL JOY is not a human experience in and of itself. REAL JOY is the spirit of God expressing Herself through us, and therefore in that moment we are touched by eternal love and opened to our own immortality. REAL JOY is the holy bridge between the finite and the infinite that changes us forever.

Moments of JOY are transformative and are meant to be so. These blessed shifts can occur at any time for any reason. By staying in our prayerful disciplines and meditative practices, we can keep ourselves closer to our spirit nature and therefore closer to God's gateway for JOY to enter into our experiences. As more JOY moments come through our daily lives, our personal and spiritual evolution accelerates. We transform. We become more God-like. We die to old limitations and are reborn to a greater version of ourselves. In a moment of REAL JOY, we step out of being simply human and become simply divine.

These transformative experiences open the eyes of our soul and show again that life is bigger than we previously thought. We actually get that stating "life is endless, we are endless" is true. Somewhere in REAL JOY, we actually felt that truth. We really get it. It makes sense now. Even the science of it becomes clear. Energy can neither be created nor destroyed. It can only be transformed. Finally, we get it. We are energy. We are God's energy! We transform endlessly every time the touch of God comes to us through REAL JOY.

REAL JOY transcends death and the false notion of its finality. REAL JOY is the homecoming to the heaven that is in our hearts. It teaches, heals, and returns us to our true nature in God, eternal love on earth as it is in heaven.

Every day can be an opportunity for REAL JOY. Every day, we can truly feel a godly connection no matter where we are. We just need to expect it and accept it is so. There is so much power in the heart that wants and waits for REAL JOY. It can change our cell tissues, our path, and our purpose in daily living. It can change lives.

The heart that holds JOY can step into any room and literally can affect everything and everyone in it. The light of JOY is God radiantly making His presence known and available.

The JOY-ful heart is a true servant of God, sometimes without knowing it. This can be the best kind of transformation. This is how God works. His ways are peaceful and never forceful.

The JOY-ful heart carries God and Her mission to bring all people back to the truth about divine love and divine living, even while we are still in the body. The JOY-ful heart who keeps a steady path of prayer, gratitude, and healing forgiveness for self and others is a new type of mystic. If we say yes to becoming JOY-ful, we become the new mystics in the marketplace. We can carry the living word of God no matter where we are or what we are doing. From washing dishes, changing a diaper, or building a deck to designing a facility for the disadvantaged, we will be carrying the eternal love of God with us. Our JOY will bring healing and success regardless of the circumstance. Most of the time, we may not be aware of the effects JOY can have, yet the results will eventually be made evident. JOY cannot fail. JOY is God's love and power and will not – cannot – fail.

REAL JOY and love is God helping us to become who we already are. Like the sunflower seed that becomes its own sunflower, REAL JOY is God's love ready to blossom from within us at any moment.

Let it be, then, that REAL JOY becomes our only purpose. Let it be that we become the JOY-ful heart who enters into any space and changes it. Let it be that we say yes to JOY and a life bathed in God's love all the time. Let it be that we choose JOY above all else, that the glory of God can be known and felt everywhere. Let it be that we make a JOY-ful noise through our lives. Let it be a bit of heaven, here and now!

REJOICE!

Remembering the JOY remedy:

* At the start of each day, ask God to enhance the light in your heart to be the brightest light no matter where you are. The effects will bring much JOY to everyone, including you!

* At the end of the day, ask God to show you how you may have touched someone's life with your JOY light and who may have touched yours.

* Allow 10 minutes during the day when you can sit comfortably and quietly. Simply observe everyone in your surroundings. Ask God to bless each one you see with great JOY. Then visualize each one with a glowing, golden light shining in his or her heart. You will notice how this increases your own JOY as well.

* At night, before going to sleep, think of someone who you may have encountered during the day that seemed to be experiencing some kind of difficulty. Sense that person and ask God to enhance the light in his or her heart with great wisdom and love so that person can find his or her way back to JOY-ful living.

* At the start of each day, before beginning your work or activities of the day look into a mirror and give yourself a very big smiling face, repeating 10 times "I am JOY. I am going to give JOY and receive JOY all day!" You will have many JOY-ful moments.

"Therefore, my heart is glad and my tongue rejoices. My body also will live in hope because you will not abandon me to the grave nor will you let your Holy One see decay. You have made known to me the paths of life. You will fill me with joy in your presence."

Acts 2:26-28

Let your life be God's signature for JOY, now and forever!

Amen, Amen, and Amen

Printed in the United States
By Bookmasters